# SAJINI'S

# POETIC

# BREEZE

**Sneak-Peek to see many Award-Winning Poems Present Inside!**

**Sajini Varadharajan**

*Ask my Amma's heart*

*For me, it always beats,*

*Ask my Appa's passion and patience*

*For me, my name, it always repeats,*

*Ask my Ammama's lips*

*For me, it always prays,*

*Ask my Thathu's wisdom and warmth*

*For me, it illuminates my path with sun's rays,*

*Ask my Patti's affection*

*For me, it's a starry shower,*

*Ask my Thatha's words of praise*

*For me, it's filled with power,*

*Ask my teachers' dedication*

*For me, it is endless nourishment!!*

*Praying for God's unending mercy,*

*He helps me accomplish the impossible...*

*People have taken Sajini's books to their heart and I hope you will too…*

"Sajini is a young, talented girl who is an inspiration to many. Her books are vibrant, thrilling and fresh. I am proud to be her teacher and have learnt a lot from her. She's a pearl, shining and making her own path!"

-Ms. Brooke D'Souza

"Sajini's books are well written, especially for her age. She's one of my biggest inspirations. Whenever I want to read a book, my hand reaches out for one of Sajini's books and it always cheers me up."

-Teresa Suresh

"Sajini's writing skills are on the next level. I've read her books. The vibrant language and new vocabulary she used in her books, it's just perfect! I love her talent and wish her a lot of success ahead!"

-Sushmita Das

"Sajini is an awesome writer, her works are imaginative and creative, and her poems are lovely to read and listen to. Her stories follow an interesting and attention-capturing plot. Looking forward to read her new books."

-Irene Sarah Robin

"I love Sajini's books. I wish I could become like her. She's one of the best young authors I've ever known. Sajini, thank you for inspiring me and thank you for writing amazing books."

-Joel Antony

# 1.    A Hidden Power

Where the blaze shines bright,

There's a hidden power in sight,

As it falls from the sky,

And disappears up so high,

From the stars it gives a gleam.


As we are showered by the power,

Each blessing in disguise is ours,

For every milestone to take,

Has the power to shake,

And change the way life goes.


The power has all the might,

To change our path in sight,

For it comes from the Almighty,

Could rewrite our destiny,

And the road to success.

# 2.   A Little Spark

In my mind shone a spark,

A spark with a little mark,

And as a part of the spark,

In the candle, in the dark,

Was a light with a glow arc.

An idea can change the day,

A life with a creative sunray,

A new imaginative world, I say,

With keen intellect, my mind plays,

Be it a storm or a blissful day.

For every problem, there's a solution,

And the brain is a closet of execution,

Each solution is an illusion,

For life is a bed of creation,

Open arms for a spark of deep
imagination.

# 3.   <u>Alone</u>

Being alone couldn't be being sad,

It's just giving yourself time to think,

Reflect or recollect events,

That fills a jug of recall drink.

Being alone isn't a punishment,

It's just that you're relaxing,

Resting and calming your nerves,

And bringing to normal your pacing.

Being alone isn't trouble,

You're spending time with yourself,

Occupying you fully in mind,

Coming up with things to delve.

Being alone is a magical moment,

Mistaken as a synonym of lonely,

Where it is you and your circle,

And showing beauty in specialty.

# 4.   Painting Skies

Painting skies of lonely bliss,

Painting skies of time,

As grey painted skies get colder,

So does the moment of mine.

Painting skies of colours,

Painting skies on the path of life,

As enchantment bubbles above,

For beauty of a portrait we strive.


Time and again paints the skies,

With memories happy and sad,

A little spice, a little sweet,

For the skies are enormously glad.

The sky likes being painted,

For everyone's skies are unique,

Paint your skies on your own,

Be it by the boat or a creek

# 5.   My Sissy Ruined My Homework

"My sissy ruined my homework,

She scribbled on it," I explained,

But when I tried to escape,

Disbelief, on my teacher, rained.


I saw my teacher's frown,

I didn't want to forget,

That if I did not excuse,

My teacher would come to a bet.


"She tore my pages out,

And cut them into strips to let,

She converted them into noodles,

With her play kitchen set."

"She poured out the ink of my pen,

And let it fall into cups, you see,

She fed it to my parents,

As thick blue tea."


"She crumpled up my math papers,

And flattened it into cakes,

Fed it to her dolls,

Cleaning up the bits with a rake."


"She wore a painted coat,

And drew crocodiles on my pages,

She would scream if I said no,

Not stopping her business for ages."

"Did she wear sissy spectacles?"

My teacher was not convinced,

"Yes," I added, "But when I snatched it,

Her paint water was all I rinsed."


My teacher raised a hand, but I spoke,

As immediately as things were,

"She placed it on an easel,

And drew thick brown fur."


"She wrote all over my backpack,

And threw it in the bin,

We had to run to the shop,

And buy a new one for kith and kin."

"Your sister who ruined your homework?"

My teacher got the benefit of doubt,

She made me repeat my homework,

For the class, standing out.


I realized I'd made a mistake,

I needn't have talked about my sister,

My homework wasn't ruined by her,

It was my own brother!

# 6.   <u>Last Sight</u>

It is my last sight of the sky,

My last sight of daylight,

My final view of dusk,

And the enduring bliss of twilight.

My last glimpse of the Moon,

Which plays games every night,

I'd like to enjoy each moment,

After all, it's the finishing sight.


It is my last wish to be,

As high up as a tree,

In the world of leaves,

I'd like to be a star, you see.

My final row of landscape,

And each step I take,

Will be the last, not the least,

It's my last sight I make.

# 7.  A Pond of Peace

A pond of peace rolls behind my castle,

It's a garden of undivided love,

Esteemed diversity crowned by a peace
dove,

The vibrant fishes in plenty bound,

Amidst the seaweeds of fresh ground,

And lotus flowers, like pink sparkles, lie
and float,

Over the mystical lake, the shiny moat,

Under the Sun, glowing like an owl's hoot,

But nothing can match the unity,

Of ducks and frogs to the west, the stars,

Gaze intensively at their eyes, who stare
above,

Into the night's milky sky cove,

Amazed with excellence and peek and
peek,

On a wild queen's lake, in wonder's see

# 8.    Blazing Dancer

A dancer of orange, a soul rekindled,

Every time a lamp comes to play,

She dances her heart out till her feet are
sore,

Indeed, she dances every day.


When called, she moves her feet,

She pulls herself to a light,

She dances with grace and glow,

A blazing fighter, with all due might.


She's a whisper in the darkness,

She's a shine in the night,

She's a colour of the rainbow,

A blazing dancer alight.

# 9. A Friend in my Mind

You are a strength, a support,

An emotional power for life,

You're the cure and you're the hurt,

You're the aim and the strive.


Being a mental buddy, you're the joy,

You're the anger, you're the fire,

That drives me to success,

Never knew I'd soar higher.


You're my best friend, you're a guide,

Who listens to all I have to say,

You bring a smile on my face,

And I'll cherish you night and day!

# 10.  Playing Sparks

A tiny mark across the sky,

I played a spark for my journey,

It was not a game, it was major,

It wasn't a joke, for me.


It was a tiny blaze of fire,

I played a wrong move,

I was near to the destination,

When I turned around the groove.


I played a spark, it's a change,

I played a spark at range,

I played a spark alight,

With all my head start might!

# 11.  Diamond

Gleaming in the light,

A part of a pendant,

An attractive section of a necklace,

It's a diamond, the attendant!


With ebullient lustre and grace,

It shines up in the sky,

It's found with endless joy,

As it brightens things up high.


It's the diamond, the form of carbon,

The hardest natural substance on Earth,

It's a glowing non-metal,

Having its own priceless worth.

# 12.  My Heart is a Lamp

I never imagined a day,

Where my own shadow,

Would travel far from me,

Up and away...


Why is my mind so lost?

Torn and destroyed are each moment,

My heart is a lamp, I stay quiet,

I can't believe, this life comes at a cost.


What does this relation mean?

It does not give or take,

My wick is soaking in oil,

And dripping each scene.

# 13.  Cast an eye

She cast an eye of rage,

She cast an eye of agony,

It was a look of pain,

In sorrow's anguished gaze.

She cast an eye of grief,

As gravity pulled her down,

Despair, distraught in life's hole,

Cold, empty and numb relief.


Her eyes exceed loneliness' arms,

That open to the dark outside,

Shades of mist across her dawn,

And dusk's wistful harms.

Worries in her soul, as drags pensive,

When sunlight turns its face,

Hovering without an aim alone,

She cast an eye expressive.

# 14.  <u>Rowing Livelihood</u>

The tails of thunder flood the sky,

Yet he survives, in the soul of the eye,

Bristles of lightning in its misty drop,

But the man is alive, floating atop.

Clouds with frozen seeds, falling gay,

Streaks of a bruise in a dark ray,

Yet, he chose to stay in a pensive route,

Clutching for life, his boat's loot,

Cotton candy releasing sugar, so bland,

Not letting them fall into his mouth's
brand,

In the depths of the sea, what dangers lie,

But, for no reason, does he say goodbye.

Violent and aggressive, fighting the storm,

Until his last breath, repeating the norm,

Rowing livelihood, willpower that thrives,

Yes, with all due courage, he survives.

# 15.  <u>Harvesting</u>

Her upbringing is soulful, her enthusiasm
mystique,

Each year, a growing crop pristine,

When harvested, she's plentiful in time,

With brightly trimmed locks, she looks just
fine.

In every direction you see, she has a
prime lily,

Pasted buds across her hair, she's a
queen,

Melodies whispering in her seeds, to
nurture all around,

Sometimes a red, or a maroon profound.

Harvesting her with threads of glory,

A cure to all, an authentic mystery,

Maybe a little sprout, will somehow soon
shine,

Misty taste of moonshine, a teardrop of
harvest in her eye.

# 16.   It's more...

It's more than just a crust,

It's more than just a pain sore...

It's more than all you see,

For every detail is more.

It's more than just a prick,

It's more than just a song,

It's more than just sadness,

Every inch of trails along.


It's more than what you think,

It's more than just a ray,

It's more than just a stake,

Every lesson has to pay.

It's more than just some distance,

Throughout life I've run,

I fall back, but I start again,

For it's more than just having fun.

# 17.   <u>Seagulls and Bread Crumbs</u>

Seagulls fly o'er the sea,

Adjacent to our dear home,

Pretty white birds,

Fluttering with wings,

They're just blissful things.

Throwing a handful of bread crumbs to
them,

They catch it so skilfully,

Grabbing the crumbs,

With all might,

They have the vigilance, day and night.

Seagulls and bread crumbs go hand in
hand,

Every meal of life's run,

Types of birds, that persevere,

Their goal is set, far or near.

# 18.  <u>When I turn king...</u>

Be I a king of film reality,

Be I a brilliant superstar,

When I turn king, I'm to be,

The most of kindness at par.

Be I the mightiest of the mighty,

Be I a soul who provides life,

When I turn king, I'm to be,

A partner for better in strive.

Be I greater than the greatest,

Be I the ruler of the world,

When I turn king, I'm to be,

Virtue-filled in equality curled!

Be I respected and loved by all,

But every step I take,

When I turn king, I'd feel proud,

Of right decisions I make.

# <u>19.   I can never feel normal...</u>

After the battle with myself,

My insides won with glee,

I lost and I can try,

But I can never feel normally,

Raging spirits within my soul,

Fighting the living tree.

Should I choose to live again?


As I follow my path's journey,

I battled in anger with my heart,

For I remain a busy bee,

But I lost, can I feel normal?

In times where I can't see.

Yes, advice would say a million times,

To never give up in times of rain,

What's most hurtful in life,

Which keeps me suffering in pain,

No matter what happens,

I can never feel normal again.

# 20.  Presence of you

It touched me and went,

What type of a feel?

Fragrance has illuminated me,

And my mind's in reel.

In happiness that surrounds me,

Perhaps I'll swoon and fall,

Unhinged it has made me,

Where love knows it all.

All my frames contain your name that goes,

See the embrace, embrace, embrace as it grows...

Here and there joy that my heart only knows,

From every breath to heartbeats alike, in moments that capture me...

Here and there I see you,

In me you reside too,

Here and there I see you,

Where and when I'll find you,

Here and there I....

Moments on this ground, it's your dream
coming alive,

Next to the river, the talk of us resides,

Entering into this zone, you've put your
feet,

We've got one power, things that include
me,

And now we'll be travelling together,

That's just one path we will follow,

Both share the same happiness, we're
best friends you see...

All my frames contain your name that
goes...

See the embrace, embrace, embrace as it
grows...

Here and there joy that my heart only
knows,

From every breath to heartbeats alike, in
moments that capture me...

Here and there I see you,

In me you reside too,

Here and there I see you,

Where and when I'll find you,

Here and there I....

# 21. The Sun

Sun, my alarm clock has not rung yet.

It's alright to rise a bit late.

It's alright to not shine on my face.

It's alright to set early.

Oh no, you've risen and woken me up.

Your gleaming yellow rays have fallen on my face.

You've woken my plants and lit up my bedroom.

Lighting the sky, lighting the trees, lighting the rooms, lighting the roads, lighting up the curtains, your journey doesn't stop –

Almighty Sun never forgives a minute late,

I may plead when nothing goes my way,

Then, let's follow punctuality every day,

Let's wake on time and complete all our chores,

Make ourselves active and disciplined like
the Sun,

Make our plan for the day,

Let's do it, and we'll want things our way,

The Sun supports those who are punctual,

And compels those who don't think,

That we should be on time, no matter
what we do,

And motivate our spirits at might.

# 22. The Seed in Bloom

Under the twilight, seeds take shape,

Their whispers soft, as they grow in bloom,

A choice to sow, a future in cape,

In dreams, our actions woven in drape,

Yet one stands out, woven in loom.

Through fields of gold, the seeds take flight,

Each kernel holds a world untold,

In every plant, a beacon bright,

In choices made, our futures alight,

The seeds we plant, our story bold.

As day dissolves, the twilight anew,

We nurture seeds of change unknown,

In memories, our actions true,

Our sustainable paths have painted beautiful hues,

In Earth's embrace, our love is sown.

# 23. The World of Women

When the sound of a girl crying echoes,

It means the sound of the Earth,

Bearing music signifying purity,

A new life, it has given birth,

In all means, women's commencing dignity.


When the sound of learning to walk is felt,

It means slow tumbling, but to persevere,

Is never taught, a symbol imbibed,

Exploring new wonders without an inch of fear,

In all means, women's growth revived.

When the sound of transitioning to a
woman is known,

It means the mighty roar of the wind
strong,

Carving a path for independence,

A change in mind, intellectual raising
along,

In all means, women's build-up of multi-
tasking sense.


When the sound of being able to earn for
all is seen,

It means the clouds clashing the air with
lightning,

A women's voice arising in the depth,

For reasons across the starry nights which
bring,

In all means, women's strength, with a
glow crept.

When the sound of celebrating women power,

To endure, to face, to love and to grow,

With a career, a wife, a mother, a sister and a daughter remarkable,

Finding all ways to never leave a single show,

To prove herself capable of doing the impossible.


Let's all rise on this auspicious occasion,

To applaud each and every woman we know,

For all they do, with tireless effort and a smile,

Which we call 'Women's Day', so,

The rainbow of the world is Women Worthwhile!

# 24. The Child's Mind – A Trailblazer of Imagination

Casting wishes on petals so small,

Chasing dreams so tall,

Imagination flies high, like a bird in the sky,

The child's mind has more than meets the eye.

A little butterfly, while floating in the air,

The thought of admiration spells up there,

Creativity soars, in every raindrop that pours,

The child's mind gushes in waves across the shores.


Rainbows that fill the sunny clouds with glee,

Colours and shades, magic brews in mystery,

A heart of pleasure, including priceless treasures,

The child's mind thinks vibrantly, without measure.

Shining in the sky, the exuberant Sun,

Under the Moon's grace, having exclusive fun,

Going after the rays, pouring joy in numerous
ways,

The child's mind, for endless moments,
happiness stays.


Dancing among the grass, as time passes by,

Enjoying the hay's scent, in hopes, they lie,

Swaying with the tree, across the gentle
breeze,

The child's mind, in all means, strives to
please.

For a world of wonder, the child begins to
grow,

Fresh flowers and nature, creativity comes to
know,

Wherever they go, sparking the wings of
compassion,

The child's mind blooms in amazement with
imagination!

# 25. My Love for the UAE – A Land of Celebration

There was once a land, new-born to
Mother Earth,

Unknown to the whispers of its dry,
enormous hearth,

At the Eastern end of the Arabian
Peninsula, it was located,

Until it was inhabited, it said, "Oh, why am
I deserted?"

With the extraordinary vision of Late H.H
Sheikh Zayed,

December 2nd 1971 became a noble
national day celebrated.

The land began to grow with its peace and purity,

As expats, citizens and nationals began to live peacefully,

With rich history, diverse nationalities, mixed communities,

Harmonious co-existence with rich opportunities.


With all the innovations, the land said with glee,

"Arabic is my traditional and cultural key!"

"Assalamu Alaikum!" a 1400-year-old Arabic greeting,

"Wa'alaykum as-salām" used for every occasion and meeting,

"Marhabaan bikum fi al'iimarat" for a tour of UAE culture,

Respect, tolerance and hospitality fills the atmosphere.

United Arab Emirates, blooming with
diverse culture and privilege,

Preserving the Ghaf Tree, Folkloric
Literature and Architectural Heritage,

Falconry, Pearl Diving, Alhaum, Horse
Racing and much more,

Technology and sustainability for future
visions, galore!


A flag of four colours, fluttering like a
beacon,

Of unity and prosperity, rising like a
falcon,

Unblemished, undeterred, a blissful sight,

Saluting UAE's emblem with a glory of
might.

COP28 and activities to nurture a greener
planet,

For goals on this 52nd National Day, the
platform is set.

"Towards the next 48" marching to UAE's century,

With a mind-blowing mission of growth, welfare and plenty,

An unending, "Long Live UAE!" round of applause we render,

To our home away from home, this ambitious futuristic splendour!

# <u>26. Flow of Hope: A Symphony of Transformation</u>

"On this Earth, where the enchanting elixir
supports life,

The vital elixir, indispensable for survival,"
I said,

Detecting the acute need for clean water
and sanitation,

Ms. SDG 6, with apprehension, shook her
head.


"From majestic peaks to lush farms, aqua
gushes,

Nature's pristine and noble offering," she
raised a brow,

"Sustainably manage and regulate Adam's
ale,

Ignite the drop of equality, the time is
now!"

"Safe and affordable drinking water, a
basic right," I replied,

Placing a water meter in every home, to
be aware,

Pledging never to squander this priceless
wealth,

Raise a global chorus, access to water we
all share."


"Arise, awake and innovate at the
earliest,"

"Stop not till the task is accomplished!"
Ms. SDG 6 mentioned,

"Small actions can indeed make a big
difference,

Clean water means good health without
tension!"


"Introducing 'Aquadon', the purifier of
water bodies,

With advanced Artificial Intelligence
features, galore,

Rainwater harvesting, desalination,
wastewater treatment, executed,

Every worthy water-related ecosystem,
restored."


"Be mindful of fostering facilities and
hygiene's might,

Sanitation is integral and vital," Ms. SDG 6
worriedly recalled,

"Heedful and attentive to the needs of
women and girls,

Secure and procure equitable sanitation
for one and all."


"Ending open defecation in every
neighbourhood,

Teaching handwashing, making it a
routine,

In every school, home and community," I
emphasized.

"Treating wastewater right, keeping
streets clean!"


"There must be a solution to this," Ms.
SDG 6 whimpered,

"To strengthen participation in sanitation
management,

Capacity-building will lend a helping hand,

Recycling and reuse technologies, a must
to avoid ailments."


"Lavines, a flying solution, for basic
sanitation," I announced,

"Planes, to cater to the needs of the
whole lot, in every town,

Until adequate amenities are designed
and implemented,

Fitted to dispose waste appropriately, in
places green, blue or brown."

"Let harmonious health, well-being and
vigor shine,

On this Unshakeable Universe, on every
mankind," Ms. SDG 6 prayed,

"Let's turn 'clean water and sanitation for
all' into reality,

Making sure we use them right, for
benefit of each, pervade!


"Overcoming collectively and mutually,
the obstacles that arise,

Towards a promising future, hand-in-hand
we proceed,

In harmony with nature, for primal bloom
and longevity,

Looking up to you Ms. SDG 6, we shall
conquer and succeed."

# <u>27. Opulent and Outstanding Odisha</u>

Known for pristine beaches, rich flora,
fauna and divine shrines,

A role model of Indian Architecture, with
heritage artistic and rich,

One of the most beautiful state in India
situated in the East,

With optimistic Odissi and Chariot
Festival, Odisha does enrich!

With forests that cover nearly one-third of
the state,

Adding to geologic formations that
prosper and flourish,

A green, cool region of tourist
destinations to enjoy,

Pakhala, Chenna Poda and Pulao,
delicacies that a tourist could wish!

An abundance of natural resources like
minerals, lakes and rivers,

Friendly and amicable visitors spark the
motivation to visit,

Sambhalpuri Sari and Dhoti, vibrant and a
colourful splendor,

A place which enchants the beauty of
every exploration minute!

The Dhauli Hills, Ratnagiri and Udayagiri
Caves to see,

Taking us to another stage of spirituality,
divinity and devotion,

A home to wildlife sanctuaries, national
parks and long-stretched coastlines,

Odisha is indeed a stream of culture and
tradition!

The next time you plan a visit to India,

Take a journey to the Opulent and
Outstanding Odisha too,

A natural beauty, a treat for all to see,

A salute to my motherland with a savvy
state, Odisha, that's true!

# 28. Happy Birthday Mom!

"Love" is a word that means a lot,

It has a connection with you,

Petals fall from the sky,

Of roses in full bloom.


Happy Birthday, you are always a special
mother,

But I recognize you as a woman,

Strong and selfless, caring and wise,

With you, victory is always driven!


Your laughter lights up our days,

In your presence, joy always stays,

With every hug and gentle touch,

I feel your love, oh so much.

# 29. Happy Birthday Grandpa!

There's a reason why you're called 'Grand'

Thank you for the fun times,

Of all the wisdom and love,

You are a guiding light,

With a smile, with a face,

Of stars shining bright.

I wish this day and upcoming years,

Full of happiness tender,

Like a beacon, you're one of a kind,

And all the 'Happy Birthday' wishes I render!

Your warmth and laughter fill our days,

In countless, heartfelt, loving ways,

May your journey ahead be filled with cheer,

Happy Birthday, Grandpa, to a year sincere!

# 30. Happy Birthday Grandma!

Her smile of beauty,

Cheers across the atmosphere,

Laughter in the walls,

Echoing all over our hearts,

Happy birthday, dear grandma!

Your wisdom shines bright,

A guiding star in the night,

Stories shared with care,

Memories beyond compare,

Happy birthday, dear grandma!

In your embrace, we find,

A love so pure and kind,

With every hug and kiss,

You bring us endless bliss,

Happy birthday, dear grandma!

# <u>31. The Blossoms of Humanity</u>

The essence of humanity,

In blossoms, takes its form,


Our moral virtues, vividly,

In society, it transforms.


The tulip's gentle compassion,

The lotus's deep concern,


Teach us to respect one another,

From these blooms, we yearn to learn.


The rose, the emblem of empathy,

The lily, kindness in full bloom,

They inspire us to share and care,

Ready to dispel others' gloom.


The sunflower's radiant humility,

The daffodil's wisdom's grace,


They remind us to bow down humbly,

In knowledge's enchanting space.


Each bloom reveals our roots,

The world yearns for more than expertise,
you see,


For souls brimming with humanity,

That's what we should aspire to be!

# <u>32. Lullaby that leads life...</u>

Listen, young one, to this lullaby,

The song which life heads still,

Be happy and positive every minute,

Good things come to you, they always will.

Listen, mighty to this lullaby,

Grow in your preference, no matter you see,

Stand for yourself and live to your expectations,

Good things come to you; in disguise they'll be.

Listen, old one, to this lullaby,

The end is always bittersweet,

Maybe it's not thoughts that tell,

Good things come to you for a treat.

It's close to nothing that we imagine,

Life paves way to gasp or sigh.

There's colour in every note we sing,

So, listen, friends, to this lovely lullaby.

# 33. Thank you, FAAH Group!

On the Women's Wing, where a group soars,

For appreciating women who make a change,

Going out of the way for a bright future,

It's the FAAH Group, on the sunshine range!

I would like to rise on this occasion,

To applaud the FAAH Group with gratitude,

For recognizing and appreciating me,

To Hasina Ma'am, I offer a sincere salute.

On this Women's Day, thank you for this awesome platform, I agree!

Your support and encouragement set us free,

Together we strive, together we achieve,

With FAAH Group's light, we all believe.

# 34. Thank You, Pudhumai Thamizhachi

A novel outlook towards talented women,

Pudhumai Thamizhachi, you show,

For every woman, you share their voice,

With an opportunity which you bestow.


Thank you, Pudhumai Thamizhachi,

For the recognition you've instilled
profound,

The gratitude I show to Dr. Sridevi,

Is limitless without any bounds!


Through your guidance, dreams come
true,

Empowering many to pursue,

A future bright, where talents gleam,

Pudhumai Thamizhachi, you inspire the
dream.

# 35. The World of Bountiful Books

Opening the doors to books,

The Pick2Read Library overlooks,

The cavern of gifts, rentals and memberships,

Sessions with expertise and writers at its tip.

An enchanted world of popular authors and series,

Book donation drives and celebrations with ease,

Competitions and events filled with glee,

An amazing platform, Pick2Read, I truly agree!

Within its walls, dreams take flight,

Pages turning day and night,

A haven for all who seek and find,

In Pick2Read, a world combined.

# 36. Clevered's Glow on my Talent

The word 'Clevered' is much more than being clever to me,

It's a journey of experience, you see,

With the Junior Data Scientist Course, I commenced,

With expert wisdom and guidance, I progressed.

Code combats, quizzes and talent hunts,

A part of my journey confronts,

Shaping my 20 books, including AI,

With my 5th and 16th book, I reached the sky!

AIIP, PIP, in my way, I soar,

Eagerly awaiting much, much more,

With my poetic talent, I say thank you,

To Clevered, for every single step is new!

# 37. Stories by Children – Thank You!

In a world where dreams take flight,

Young minds crafting pure delight,

With every word, a new adventure,

Stories by Children, a wondrous venture.

Thank you so much for this chance,

To join in the creative dance,

For bringing to light my novel's spark,

Illuminating paths in the dark.

I hope to be an integral part,

And explore creativity instrumental,

Together we'll weave tales from the heart,

Inspiring futures, bright and monumental!

# 38. A Simple Life

You would ask me a question,

When you read this title,

What's the actual point?

Of leading a life so simple...

I'll answer that question for you,

Complex networks in our paths,

Leave us in daze and difficulty,

To mind-map the process arts.

Each change that we invite,

May be wanted or unworthy,

Keep moving on a straight path,

And diverge without question on paths curvy.

Lead a life simple, for every note we strike,

Bring about a difference in ways,

A great difference, maybe a development,

Simple lives have much more growth to gaze!

# 39. Life without change...

Life without change, does it have
meaning?

The breeze whispered in my ears,

Is it a period of transition?

Or does it mean signals over years?

Is it a time of discussion?

It's a question left unanswered in peers.

Until I saw my mother, I'd assumed there
was no Almighty,

Until I started seeing dreams, I'd assumed
there was no desire,

Until I felt the pull, I knew there was no
change,

Until I'd written poetry, I'd felt there was
no meaning to life's fire.

Until I'd seen the rivers and the lakes, I
felt there was no sea,

And transitions had made their mark into
the bliss of trees.

If there would have been no life, there
would be no Earth,

If there wouldn't have been words, there
would be no language,

Until there was no embrace, there
would've been no star,

Until there was a fragrance, there
would've been no flower's gaze,

If there was not a chirp, there would've
been no birds,

And if there were no letters, there
would've been no words.

Life without change, does it have
meaning?

The breeze whispered in my ears,

Is it a period of transition?

Or does it mean signals over years?

Is it a time of discussion?

It's a question left unanswered in peers.

# <u>40. True Friendship Means...</u>

A close bond of friendship, at the coffee table,

With warm steaming mugs, a discussion it enables,

Cherished memories, three friends begin to recall,

Laughing with pleasant smiles, back in time to enthrall.

As young girls, having jewels and beads in hand,

Putting their bonds into a strong, significant stand,

Friendships beginning, with jewellery made,

Into bracelets and necklaces, closer together in braid.

Smiles and joy as they fill the air with happiness,

Lovely stories of their youth in childishness,

With bracelets in their hands, they symbolize no parting,

A deepening companionship, slow-paced starting.

As they grow older, the jewellery reminds of the early,

With hands together, their promise is fastened securely,

Never to leave each other's side, no matter the situation,

Embrace things together, like bracelets' excavation.

Sharing hugs as they continue their older journey of life,

To remain attached forever, they always strive,

Lives that they share, through thick and thin,

But in the end, a true friendship is what always wins.

# 41. Motherly Colours

If I should die, think only this of me,

Somewhere in the depth of the heart, I reside,

The memories that remind you, that you still see,

In every part of your house, I'm always by your side,

From the time you were a child, did you have a thought?

Held in my hands, the gift of affection and encouragement,

We made a long journey, the battles that we together fought,

Gushing waves that tell stories of motherly achievement.

Make note, this piece, shall stay with you for days,

It beats in your inner soul, in your feelings so deep,

Get it back, get the whispers of my voice
in your ears,

My vision for you, I'm more concerned
than your mind says,

My smile has caused your peace and
happiness in keep,

My wistful looks are what bring oceans of
tears.

# WELCOME TO THE HAIKU SECTION!

# 42. Sweet Haikus

Oh, my dear flower,

Are you talking to me?

Nod your head and see.

A little sweet fruit,

In my mouth the nature juice,

And essence to use.


A gleaming lantern,

In the sky shining above me,

A yellow power.

May be of phases,

Playing a game inside out,

Sweet dreams in a spout.

Gush and rush and soar,

Nature's mystique construction,

Dancing on the shore.

# 43. Rise and Shine Haikus

Sunrise up in start,

Birds singing songs to glory,

Dew drops on the leaves.

Cold snow pellets' tree,

White on the ground all over,

Each mile with flakes falls.

Carrying honey,

The little bees flutter,

In the air they hover.

On the leaves, water,

Early morning, they condense,

As dew drops prudence.

With green leaves they stand,

Branches spread like fairyland,

A sight of nature.

# 44. Instrumental Haikus

The black and white keys,

Are brought to life with music,

With fingers on time.

Strings to pluck music,

Each string has a special chord,

Uniqueness it shows.

Blow into it for sound,

A pitch, a symbol, a guide,

Every band it's a part.

A bit of blow-in,

Sweet honey-like melody,

For all to enjoy.

Art or music forms,

That whisper from the soul's core,

In the bliss of peace.

# 45. Animal Haikus

It purrs and meows,

In the backyard on the fence,

It jumps and climbs too.


I saw a brown deer,

Hopping its way, a lone path,

Going to its group.


Chirping happily,

Singing a beautiful song,

Sitting on a tree.


Galloping swiftly,

Skies filled with its power new,

A symbol of courage.

# 46. Food and Happiness Haikus

Flavours it can have,

Vegetables to plain pizza,

A treat to enjoy!


White sauce to red taste,

Penne, Fusilli, called in ways,

Italian taste!


Top with cheese or jam,

The crust and middle of joy,

A treat to enjoy!


A smile on your face,

Spreads positivity round,

Happiness, the key.

# 47. Daily Usage Haikus

Of varied genres,

Sneak-peek with an open mind,

Sitting on the rack.


Blocking the Sun rays,

No need to cry out for heat,

Protecting always.


Look in it and see,

Everything appears closely,

Distant objects be.


Grey and white colours,

Where automobiles travel,

Zebra cross to see.

Quiet, green village,

Not busy like a small bee,

Time buzzes slowly.


A soul, kind and wise,

A profession to give respect,

Make our lives worthwhile.


White doves represent,

A symbol of harmony,

To live peacefully

# 48. Light-up Haikus

Express thoughts in words,

A palace of solitude,

Poetry's endless grace.

Torch beam's keen embrace,

A panel of purity,

To show us our way.

Desert sands' embrace,

Skyscrapers touch the blue sky,

UAE's grace shines.

Words whisper on bound,

Knowledge, dreams and tales plenty,

Books' vibrant embrace.

Pursuing talent,

And achieving excellence,

Nurturing young minds.

A crystal gleaming,

Radiating keen power,

Ebullient heart.

# 49. Futuristic Haikus

The world of robots,

Speaks with technology's touch.

Intelligence peeks.


As the future binds,

A green hearth let us nurture,

To prosper always.


The majestic hearth,

Amidst the encircling gloom,

Magical portrait.


Connection of hearts,

Braving the magic that's lost,

Willpower to find.

# 50. Watchful Haikus

Once a drop today,

Will turn to ocean tomorrow,

Tranquil forever.


Yellow sands arise,

The human eyes play a game,

With crystal water.


Illusion as called,

Illustrations in real life,

Reality's page.


More to go for life,

A never-ending circle,

Road's endless embrace.

# 51. Haikus for Life

The starting of birth,

The seven stages of life,

We go back to dust.

It means no worries,

For the rest of your new days,

Stay calm and be wise.


By chance it's pleasant,

A clash to remember too,

Vacant or pensive.

Orange vicious bite,

Standing on top of the world,

Roaring like a king,


It's my last sight play,

My final row of landscape,

"Goodbye World!", I say!

# THE

# END

## **ABOUT THE AUTHOR**

"Pen + Paper = Paradise"

Sajini was awarded a place in India Book of Records, Asia Book of Records and Arabian World Records for "Maximum books written by a child." She was also awarded many prizes by 'Stories by Children' for her Novels, Themed Poems and Short Stories.

She has her own YouTube Channel on her name where she publishes her own short stories and poems for young children. She aspires to be an ecologist and wishes to open a school named, "Dream and Create School" with branches in almost every country on the globe.

When she is not writing on her desk, Sajini spends most of her time reading and narrating stories which gives wings to her imagination and creativity. She loves playing on her keyboard and coding on her computer as well. She yearns to spread kindness, peace, harmony and human values through her writing to make the Earth a wonderful place to live in! Sajini also aspires to become an entrepreneur of her own publishing company 'Writedale' to encourage young authors publish their book. You can find Sajini's books on Amazon.

Be sure to check out my other books!

www.ingramcontent.com/pod-product-compliance
Lightning Source LLC
Chambersburg PA
CBHW031758150726
47989CB00006B/2776